THIS WAY UP

A flat-pack guide to marketing the Arts
Caroline Griffin

Ａ audiences central   Commissioned from Audiences Central by AMA and Arts Council England

ACKNOWLEDGEMENTS

This book has been produced with the help and support of many people. The author would like to thank Amy Clarke and Johnathan Branson for their hard work, especially on compiling the case studies. Thanks also go to everyone who read and advised on early drafts, particularly Amy Clarke, Anita Dinham, Rachel Harrison, Simon Heath, Paul Kaynes and Vishalakshi Roy and the Reading Group – Rehana Amin, Art Asia; Simon Bedford, Hoipolloi; Kara Chatten, Wolsey Art Gallery; Lisa Craddock, Salamander Tandem; Rachel Emmett, Dance4; and Jason Grant, Apples and Snakes.

Thanks also go to everyone who helped us by providing a case study for the book: Clare Thomas, Heart 'n Soul; Chris Brown, g39; Jackie Newbould, Birmingham Contemporary Music Group; Shona McLean, Trinity Arts; Mark Dobson, Tyneside Cinema; Rehana Amin, Art Asia; Vivienne Perry, Sin Cru; Sally Rew, HamFisted!; Frederica Notley, Pop-Up; Julie Davies, Wolverhampton Art Gallery and Ranjit Atwal, The Old Town Hall, Hemel Hempstead

More information about these organisations can be found on their websites:

Heart 'n Soul www.heartnsoul.co.uk (see p.13)

G39 www.g39.org (see p.14)

Birmingham Contemporary Music Group www.bcmg.org.uk (see p.23)

Trinity Arts www.west-lindsey.gov.uk/ section.asp?catId=559 (see p.29)

Tyneside Cinema www.tynecine.org (see p.32)

Art Asia www.artasia.org.uk (see p.32)

Sin Cru www.sincru.co.uk (see p.33)

HamFisted! www.hamfisted.org.uk (see p.38)

Pop-Up www.pop-up.net (see p.39)

WAG www.wolverhamptonart.org.uk/ wolves (see p.41)

Old Town Hall www.oldtownhall.co.uk (see p.47)

CONTENTS

 YOU DO IT

HOW TO USE THIS GUIDE

This book provides you with a practical <u>hands-on guide</u> to writing a marketing plan. It is aimed at people working in small organisations with limited marketing resources, and at people who aren't marketing specialists – although marketing may be a key part of their role.

You can go from start to end to follow the individual stages to complete your plan, or you can dip in and out, picking up the sections that are most relevant to you. At the back you will find exercises, suggestions for further reading, a suggested outline for a marketing plan and a sample marketing plan to refer to.

Here are some suggestions for using the guide:

I'm interested in the very basics	Read the text of the book, but leave out the **Hints&Tips**, **You Do It** and **Take It Further** sections.
I want to prepare a working plan quickly	Use your own responses to the **You Do It** sections scattered through the text to build up the key parts of your working plan.
I want to prepare a detailed plan that agrees with everyone	Work through the book completing the **You Do It** sections with other members of your team. Use the **Hints &Tips** to add detail to your plan. There are **Hints & Tips** sections that suggests ways to help get your team working with you to produce the plan.
The full works	Complete all the sections and use the **Hints & Tips** and **You Do It** sections to ensure that your plan is thoroughly researched and presented. Follow up detailed elements of the plan in other publications using the **Taking It Further** references.

Throughout this book we have used the word 'audience' as a cover-all to describe the people that you are hoping to attract. According to your organisation and the work you do, you might usually use a different term, such as participant, visitor, stakeholder, customer or client. The principles of marketing planning are the same whichever term you use, so if audience isn't the right word for you, substitute it with one that is.

MARKETING PLAN STRUCTURE

1 WHAT'S IN IT FOR ME?

In this chapter we will be looking at the benefits a marketing plan will bring you and your organisation

Your marketing plan is a document that outlines the <u>audiences you want to attract and how you go about attracting them</u>. Its purpose is to ensure that your communications with audiences are clear and consistent and will help your organisation achieve its aims.

HAVE YOU EVER EXPERIENCED ANY OF THESE COMMON PROBLEMS?

We've got a fantastic new exhibition coming up. It should attract new audiences – but we don't know who they are . . .

The plan will help take the guesswork out of marketing.

- You will have a clearer idea of who your audiences are and what they like
- You will be able to identify what elements of your product will most appeal to your potential audiences

There's just a few days before the show and hardly any tickets sold . . . WHAT CAN WE DO?!

The plan will help you avoid the last-minute panic.

- You will have clear objectives and a timetable so you can track your campaign's success and take action early
- You'll have implemented different marketing activities and selected target groups well in advance, and you'll know which audiences will respond to last-minute approaches

The director said this artist was a hit at last year's festival, so we can expect high demand. I'm not so sure, but as I wasn't here then . . .

The plan will build in mechanisms so you can learn from your experience.

- You'll set realistic and achievable targets that can make you all feel good when you achieve them
- You'll record information that will help the organisation to plan its next campaign

HOW WILL ONE PLAN MAKE SUCH A DIFFERENCE?

A marketing plan is a straightforward tool that encourages you to think ahead, have a clear idea of your objectives and provide you with a practical action plan to achieve them.

The length, complexity and depth of a marketing plan will vary, depending on what you need it for. However detailed the plan is, it will need to cover four basic areas:

1. an overview of your project or activity and how it fits into your areas of expertise and experience

2. a consideration of what it is about your activity that will appeal to its potential audiences or consumers, alongside a consideration of who those audiences might be

3. a practical campaign plan that draws on this information and that includes a timetable and budget

4. a section that outlines how you will manage your marketing activity and how you will know that you have been successful.

By focusing your attention on these issues, and taking the time to develop them into a structured and practical plan, you will be able to imagine, define and achieve marketing success.

HOW AM I GOING TO FIND TIME TO DO ALL THIS PLANNING?

Taking time out from **doing** things so that you can plan things often seems daunting, especially when you are working in a small organisation without many staff resources, and with tight deadlines. What you need to remember is that investing a bit of time upfront into the marketing plan will, undoubtedly, save you time and money in the long run.

HOW CAN THIS BE TRUE?

It's because, at its heart, this is what marketing is all about.

Here is a straightforward definition of what marketing is:

MARKETING IS A THINKING AND PLANNING PROCESS THAT MAKES SURE YOU SPEND YOUR TIME AND MONEY ON THE RIGHT TASKS TO ACHIEVE YOUR AUDIENCE OBJECTIVES.

So, marketing isn't just about leaflets or websites (although they are important). It's about establishing some clear ideas about who you want to come (and how many of them, and how much they'll pay). More than that, it's about a set of tools that will help you achieve this in the easiest and most cost-effective way.

FLATPACK PLANNING

The processes that are laid out in this book can be equally applied to developing a plan for an organisation, for a year-long set of campaigns, or an individual campaign for one piece of work. This book will provide you with step-by-step support to develop a plan that suits you, your organisation and your current needs.

WHERE ARE WE NOW?

In this chapter we will be defining what your organisation wants to achieve and what role your audience might have in helping you reach your goals.

WHY ARE WE HERE?

Your marketing plan starts with your organisation and what it is you hope to achieve. Being clear about the 'bigger picture' will underpin and inform your marketing activity.

 YOU DO IT

WHO WE ARE

You are likely to already have a written vision or mission statement for your organisation. If you have, great, it's the starting point for your plan. If you haven't, it's time to get the team together to see if you can agree on exactly what you're here for. Discuss what you do, who it's for, and where, when and why you do it. Ensure you include your aspirations for the organisation.

[**REFER TO 1.1 OF SAMPLE MARKETING PLAN P. 61**]

It's much easier for your audiences to engage with you if you are clear and consistent about what you do and why you do it. They don't necessarily expect you to do the same thing over and over again, but they do expect your values to be transparent and consistent. A strong identity encourages trust and respect. If your audience trust you they will frequently be prepared to take risks in what they attend or see.

This identity is built up by your values, attitudes, passions, aspirations, approach and ideals. If your whole organisation shares these characteristics, you can use them to underpin all of your communications with audiences and potential audiences.

WHAT MAKES US DIFFERENT FROM EVERYBODY ELSE?

The elements that make up your organisation's character are often known as your 'brand values'. These values should underpin everything you do, across the whole organisation. If you pride yourself on being 'friendly and approachable', your customers would lose faith in the organisation if they were spoken to rudely or in an unhelpful way when they phoned for information on your next event, even if they have a great experience when they visit in person.

CASE STUDY

"Heart 'n Soul is founded on quality, integrity and diversity – principles we apply as much to our audiences' experience as to the art itself. We want to give people with learning disabilities, who often don't get access to the arts, the most exceptional and inspiring experience possible."
Clare Thomas, Heart 'n Soul

CASE STUDY

"g39 is an artist-led gallery space that exists to support emerging visual artists from across Wales and further afield. Our main objective is to provide opportunities for these artists, and we are supported by the Arts Council of Wales to do this through a programme of exhibitions in our permanent gallery venue and in non-gallery spaces."
Chris Brown, g39

 YOU DO IT

WHAT OUR AUDIENCE THINKS OF US:

In the Resource Pack (p.54) you will find a tool for working with your team to establish your existing brand values (what people think about your organisation) and the values you aspire to (what you want them to think about you).

[**REFER TO 1.2 OF SAMPLE MARKETING PLAN P. 61**]

(These brand values will come in useful again later, when planning your marketing activities, see p.36)

Distinctiveness encourages audiences to choose you over others. For example, an individual who wants to see contemporary visual art will probably choose a gallery that specialises in that, over a gallery with a more general offer.

The idea that there is something that makes your organisation different to all others is encapsulated in the idea of the USP (Unique Selling Proposition). Your USP is a phrase that describes the one key thing that makes you who you are and which no one else can lay claim to. Your USP is rarely a public statement. Its main function is to focus your whole organisation, reinforcing the things that make you distinctive in the eyes of your audiences.

 YOU DO IT

WHAT OUR AUDIENCE THINKS OF US

In a group discuss what it is that your audiences most value about your activity. Push the group to look past the obvious, such as "we provide an opportunity to see theatre"; instead, focus on those elements that influence the decisions made by customers, such as the type of work, the physical environment, the atmosphere, the facilities or the educational or social benefits. Reality check – is this something unique to your organisation?

You should now be in a position to form a brief statement that encapsulates these distinctive features.

[**REFER TO 1.2 OF SAMPLE MARKETING PLAN P. 61**]

WHO ARE MY COMPETITORS?

It is usually straightforward to identify your key direct competitors (e.g. other arts organisations, other educational opportunities). However, when making your marketing plan it is also useful to think about other organisations or activities that might be competing for your audience. Consider your audiences' social, educational or lifestyle needs and where else they might be able to get them fulfilled. For example, they may go to the theatre mainly to socialise with friends – where else might they find an opportunity to do this? (You may find it helpful to refer to the section on p.31, and use this information to refine your thinking about competitors).

 YOU DO IT

WHAT'S HAPPENING AROUND US:

Think about the various activities you want to promote to audiences. Ask yourself what else they could be doing with the time and what else they might spend their money on.

Split the competitors into two lists:

Direct competitors – a straightforward choice between you or someone else doing something very similar

Indirect competitors – a choice between you and something quite different

For example, a Saturday morning performance for children might compete with:

Direct competitors

A gallery visit to a child-friendly exhibition

A drama class

Singing in a choir

Indirect competitors

Home activities (watching TV, reading a book, surfing the internet)

Shopping with family

Formal or informal sports activities

Play date with school friends

[**REFER TO 1.3 OF SAMPLE MARKETING PLAN P. 62**]

BRINGING IT ALL TOGETHER

The information we have gathered so far includes internal and external factors that impact on your organisation. A useful way to summarise this information is to pull it together in a SWOT analysis. SWOT stands for Strengths, Weaknesses, Opportunities and Threats. This will help produce a summary of areas that your organisation should concentrate on developing.

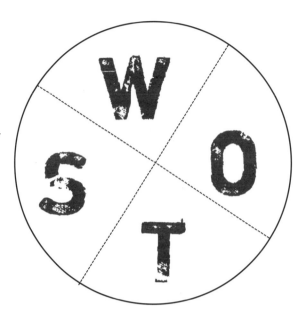

 YOU DO IT

OUR STRENGTHS, WEAKNESSES, OPPORTUNITIES AND THREATS:

Answer these to construct your **SWOT**

Strengths

What's good about your organisation?

What are the positives about the staff team, the programme, your infrastructure?

Where do you have good practice?

Where can you rely on support from your audiences?

Weaknesses

What's not so good about the organisation?

Where is there uncertainty about staffing, the programme, your infrastructure?

Where might your processes need to be improved?

Where might you be losing the support of your audiences or not be reaching audiences you want?

Opportunities

Who supports your work now? Will they continue to do so?

Where is there a good match between current or potential funders' priorities and your work?

Are there are any forthcoming political, environmental, social, technological or legislative changes that might benefit your company?

Threats

Who are your competitors?

Who are you struggling to communicate with - locally, regionally and nationally?

Where are there uncertainties about your funding or other income generation?

Are there are any forthcoming political, environmental, social, technological or legislative changes that might impact negatively on your company?

Bring the SWOT together with a brief summary of the key issues you have identified.

[**REFER TO 1.4 OF SAMPLE MARKETING PLAN P. 63**]

HINTS&TIPS

YOUR LEGAL RESPONSIBILITIES

All organisations need to take into account legislation that affects the way you treat people you come into contact with. As part of the preparation for your marketing planning process you should make sure you are aware of the impact of legislation that aims to prevent discrimination by race, age, religion or gender. You should also consider other relevant legislation including Equal Opportunities and the Safety of Children and Young People.

Your organisation may have policies that set out how you aim to comply with this legislation, for example an Equal Opportunities Policy or a Race Equality Action Plan, which should also be referred to when drawing up your plan.

Your board is responsible for ensuring that an organisation meets its legal requirements. Get them involved in your marketing planning to ensure that any legal obligations are met. Your local arts council, local authorities and specialist support agencies can offer additional assistance.

TAKING IT FURTHER

The more information you can contribute to your SWOT analysis the more useful it will be. There are more internal and external factors that are worth considering for a more detailed SWOT.

Refer to:

Peter Verwey *Marketing Planning*
Section A1–A10

Stephen Cashman *Thinking Big*
Section B 'Strategic Analysis'

3 WHERE DO WE WANT TO BE?

In this chapter we will be looking at how you choose the approaches you will take to attract your target audiences. We will also consider ways to approach developing new audiences while also working with your regular customers.

WHERE DO WE WANT TO BE IN THE FUTURE?

To start the plan we need to identify some marketing objectives for your organisation. These are practical targets that relate directly to the vision for your organisation that you identified earlier (see p. 13).

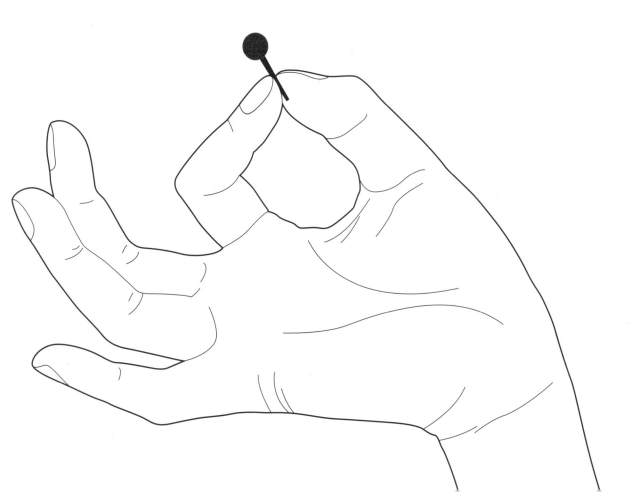

There are three primary types of objectives that tend to apply to arts organisations: artistic, social or financial. Most organisations will have a strong focus on one of these three areas, while additional objectives in the other two areas provide a healthy balance.

HINTS&TIPS

SETTING SMART OBJECTIVES

Useful objectives are specific about the outcomes you hope to achieve. Try to put precise defining statements in each objective you write. Working in a team will help identify shared goals and an understanding of each individual's role in achieving them.

Good objectives are **SMART.** This is an acronym that helps you remember what sort of parameters you should include in your objectives to ensure that they can be achieved and measured.

S	Specific	Be as precise as possible. Make sure all elements of the objective are clear. For example, if you use the term 'young people', define what you mean by that.
M	Measured·	Include a measure for your success. Common measures are number of visits, amount of money or number of individual visitors.
A	Achievable	Ensure that the targets you are setting can be delivered with the time and resources available. Make sure that you aren't committing to stretching your resources too thin at this stage. You will need some slack for things that change along the way.
R	Realistic	This is where a team contribution could really help. Make sure everyone agrees on the objectives and they're happy to make the necessary contribution to achieving them.
T	Timetabled	Put a timescale on the achievement of the target. Are you going to reach your objectives in the next week, the next year or the next three years? You might have a mix of all of these.

A good place to start when identifying objectives is to look at your mission or vision statements, or any other documents that set out the ethos and aspirations of the organisation. Your marketing objectives should pick out those elements that relate to the organisation's relationship to audiences and stakeholders. You can also use your SWOT analysis to make sure that your objectives help you to play to strengths and to compensate for or build up weak areas (see p.16).

 YOU DO IT

WHERE WE'RE HEADING

Identifying marketing objectives is the first stage in writing your marketing plan. See if you can put together a few objectives, using what you know about the organisation and what it exists to achieve (refer to your summary of the organisation; see p.13).

Make sure you have a mix of social, artistic and financial objectives. Work with other members of your team to ensure everyone agrees that achieving these objectives would reflect the organisation's aspirations for the future.

[**REFER TO 2.1 OF SAMPLE MARKETING PLAN P. 64**]

HOW DO WE ENSURE WE ACHIEVE OUR OBJECTIVES?

Imagine you need to visit a city some way away from where you live. Having decided where you are going and why you want to go there, you will start to plan how to get there.

YOU COULD:

Drive This may take a while but allow you to enjoy the scenery on the way. You might also visit an elderly relation en route, getting more value from your trip.

OR

Fly You want to get there quickly and back in the same day. This is a more expensive option but worth it for the time benefits you gain.

OR

You might contact your friend and invite them to visit you instead. This might be the right approach if you don't like travelling, can't afford it or are just very lazy.

Selecting a marketing strategy is a similar process. It is a way of deciding which approach will be most effective and efficient in helping you achieve your identified objectives.

WHAT DOES A MARKETING STRATEGY LOOK LIKE?

Broadly your routes to achieving the targets you identified in the previous chapter are likely to fall into one of two main areas:

1. to maintain and grow relationships with existing audiences, or

2. to form relationships with new audiences.

In this context the term 'new audiences' refers to new market segments rather than to new individuals from market segments you are already successful in attracting (see p. 28 for the section on market segments).

Arts organisations are often more focused on new audiences than counterpart commercial organisations are. This is usually because arts organisations have social objectives that place an emphasis on providing broad access to our work.

EXISTING AUDIENCES ARE:	NEW AUDIENCES ARE:
reliable	the regular audiences of the future
likely to attend frequently	fresh and excited about your activities
likely to be your highest spenders	likely to help you meet your social objectives
comfortable with your product	
comfortable with your communications	
relatively cheap to communicate with	

The most successful marketing plans will incorporate strategies for both audience types as both are important to you. The approaches that you are likely to take in order to attract audiences to your events are likely to fall in one or more of the following three groups:

1. MORE OF THE SAME	Keep on delivering the same sorts of activities for the same sort of people.
2. CHANGE YOUR PRODUCT	Change or alter your activities in order to attract more people from existing target groups, or entirely new target groups. (This isn't just about changing your artistic product. Think about 'product' in the broadest sense, including your facilities, added extras, and bar and catering facilities. See p. 22.)
3. DEVELOP YOUR MARKET	Bridge the gap between you and your target (new audience) groups by understanding and responding to their needs.

You might be thinking about changing both your product and your audience base. This would be a completely different approach that we could call 'doing something completely new'. This can be an extremely risky venture as it moves away from all the areas where you are solidly established. Consider whether you can achieve your ends more gradually by either focusing on product development or market development in the first instance.

MORE OF THE SAME

This strategy helps to:	• keep your audience numbers high • keep your operation cost-effective
Employ this strategy to:	• bring in a reliable income • cement deeper relationships with people you are familiar with
The benefits are:	• you are well established • you need to ensure audience visits and financial income
The downsides are:	• you use few resources for a high return • outcomes are fairly reliable and predictable • it won't diversify your audience • it may feel predictable and uninspiring

CHANGE YOUR PRODUCT

This strategy helps to:	• attract new audiences • inspire and challenge existing audiences • energise and challenge the organisation
Employ this strategy when:	• audiences you should be attracting are elusive • when there is flexibility within your organisation to make changes
The benefits are:	• you grow and expand your area of competence • you build new audiences for the long term
The downsides are:	• changing your product can be a challenging process for the team • the process can be time-consuming • change is risky

DEVELOP YOUR MARKET

This strategy helps to:	• increase the range of people attending • develop relationships with new target audiences
Employ this strategy when:	• you think audiences would benefit from extra ways to find out about you • you think that there are significant market segments who have a high probability of enjoying your work
The benefits are:	• increased audiences • meeting funding requirements for new audiences or broader audiences
The downsides are:	• it's relatively time intensive • it may be costly

It is helpful to refer back to the marketing objectives you established right at the start of this process, to ensure that the broad strategies you adopt will help you meet your aims. For example, if your main focus is developing audiences from socially excluded groups, you would probably need to work on developing the market and changing your product.

CASE STUDY

"One of our key objectives is to provide people, young and not so young, with opportunities to hear top-quality contemporary music. Concerning young people, we know they'll come to our usual concert venues if we think carefully about how to get them there and create an environment in which they feel comfortable. They'll enjoy exactly the same pieces as our regular audience, given the right consideration (e.g. involvement in a previous learning project about the pieces in the programme, front row seats at the concert, special 'young people-friendly' concert programmes, their own special interval reception). We never adapt the music programme to what we think they'll particularly like – we don't need to. Having said that, we think carefully about the presentation of the music and in addition to our concerts for mixed audiences we have developed a new strand of family concerts which engage very young children by the additional elements of theatre, film and digital media."

Jackie Newbould, Birmingham Contemporary Music Group

BUILDING RELATIONSHIPS

By and large people don't like to feel they are being 'sold to'. Marketing activity that is poorly targeted or misunderstands the needs of consumers is interpreted as a cynical attempt to deceive a customer for the purposes of making a sale, whether or not it is something the consumer wants – a perception that is neatly summed up when people talk about marketing being about "selling ice to Eskimos."

This is a misconception of the role of marketing, as it is evident that you might be able to mis-sell to someone once, but you probably can't do it again. Successful organisations have happy customers who come back time and again. They achieve this by forming relationships with their customers that encourage trust to develop.

This "relationship marketing" approach is very powerful for arts organisations. It helps develop a long-term stable core of loyal customers who can support the organisation by their attendance, their money and their active involvement.

Developing relationships with customers, participants, audiences or visitors can take many different forms. Things you might like to consider include:

Reward customer loyalty

e.g. subscription or membership-type schemes which offer financial incentives to book upfront for more events

Encourage customers to feel part of your organisation or to deepen their involvement

e.g. special events such as opportunities to meet performers

Listen to your customers

e.g. make changes to your facilities based on customer feedback

Make your customers feel that they are important as individuals

e.g. write to them after their first visit to welcome them to your organisation

 YOU DO IT

HOW WE'LL GET THERE

Revisit your SMART objectives. To achieve them will you be doing More of the Same, Developing your Market or Developing your Product? If you have any that involve working with new products and new markets, you should provide evidence of how the organisation will support this new venture.

[**REFER TO 2.2 OF SAMPLE MARKETING PLAN P. 65**]

TAKING IT FURTHER

Selecting strategic direction is an integral part of any marketing planning exercise. It can be carried out in much more detail than suggested here.

Refer to:

Stephen Cashman *Thinking Big*
Section C 'Making and Selecting Strategies'

Malcolm McDonald *Marketing Plans*
Chapter 6, p. 243

4

GETTING TO KNOW OUR AUDIENCES

In this chapter we'll think about what it is that motivates people to attend the arts and how you can communicate with them most effectively.

EVERYONE'S AN INDIVIDUAL. AREN'T THEY?

Marketing processes rely on a basic assumption that groups of people tend to be interested in the same sort of things, and act in similar ways.

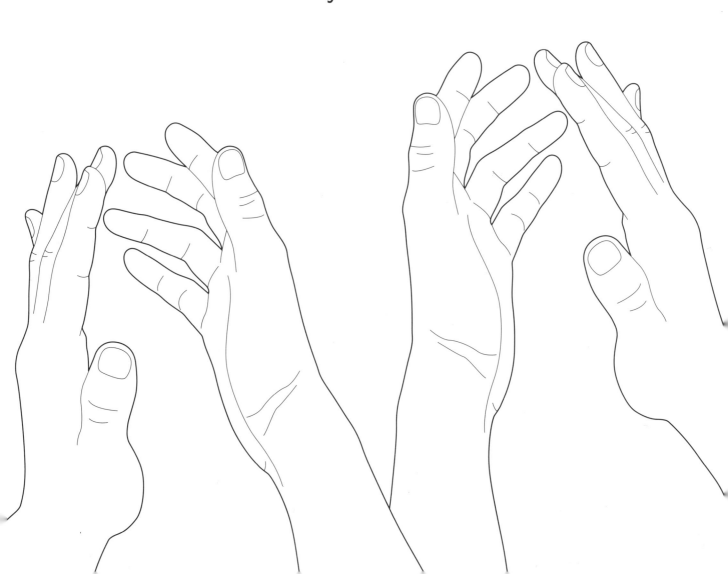

By identifying commonalities that are relevant to your organisation you can tailor your message to different groups of people and remain confident that you are speaking to them about the right things and in the right way.

THE COMMONALITIES THAT WE LOOK FOR TEND TO FALL INTO ONE OF THE FOLLOWING CATEGORIES:

Life stage	People's lifestyles are affected by where they are on their journey through life. The key areas to consider are their family circumstances (e.g. whether or not they have children and how old the children are) and their work or career path (e.g. at what stage are they in their education or in their career).
Demographics	An individual's interests and choices are determined, to some degree, by their social and educational backgrounds. Things to consider include their previous exposure to arts activity, opportunities to participate and whether attending the arts is usual among their peers.
Attitudes, values and behaviour	Spirituality, morality and values all have a significant effect on an individual's daily choices. People who are interested in environmental issues or politics or who share an outlook on life (e.g. associate with a sub-culture) will have commonalities that may affect their arts attendance. Look out for what people are already doing that might relate to your offer.
Geographical location	People with broadly similar attitudes, life stages and social and educational backgrounds tend to live in similar houses and congregate together. For this reason, postcodes are often used to identify audience groups. You can also consider the ease of travel and how long the journey might be from their home or from their workplace.

HINTS&TIPS

MARKET SEGMENTATION

Splitting audiences into distinct groups is known as identifying a 'market segment'. It is a key technique in developing cost-effective marketing activity.

Sometimes people feel uncomfortable separating people into groups in this way as it can feel like stereotyping them. Effective identification of target groups avoids this by associating people according to things that really matter to them as individuals.

Dividing your audience solely by age, ethnic background, gender, sexuality or disability can cause offence and is likely to be ineffective. These categories are too broad to define a useful target group. You can use these factors to further refine an identified segment.

For example, if your organisation has identified a desire to develop BME (black and minority ethnic) audiences, you can break this down by thinking about who these people really are. Ask yourself:

about their family circumstance

their educational background

their career and work aspirations

the things they are interested in

what they care about

what else they do

what their specific ethnic background is

what languages are spoken at home

All these factors will help you build up a much more detailed vision of the desired audience. You will know who they are and that will help tailor your messages. It will also help the audience feel that you really care about and understand them, and that you aren't being tokenistic in your approach.

HOW DO I DECIDE WHICH AUDIENCES TO FOCUS ON?

Even if a piece of work is aimed primarily at attracting new audiences to your work, it is sensible to spend some time on ensuring that your existing audiences know about the event. These people already have a relationship with you, will be relatively cost effective to communicate with, and will require less investment of time and money. If you don't include them they might feel left out! Also they can be relied upon to come with a positive outlook, which will improve the atmosphere and experience for everyone.

CASE STUDY

"The Programme Champions scheme is a successful element of the Centre's programming policy. It enables members of the local community with a particular enthusiasm (e.g. folk music) to provide recommendations for programming directly into the venue. These Programme Champions also generate interest in the local community for these events, spreading word-of-mouth and encouraging participation. Programme Champions provide an opportunity for the Centre to develop other areas of relative weakness in its programming and audience."

Shona McLean, Trinity Arts

At the start of this planning process you developed a set of marketing objectives (see p. 20). These objectives will inform your decisions about what sort of audiences you want to attract for a particular piece of work.

Accurate information is helpful in demonstrating to stakeholders and funders that they should support your activity. They will be more likely to support you if they feel that:

- you are bringing something new to your area or the art-form (which will create a new audience for itself), or

- you can fulfil an audience need that is currently unfulfilled (which will supply a gap in arts provision).

MARKET OPPORTUNITY	EVIDENCE
A previous similar event was over-subscribed	• Use your box office data or visitor records for the previous event • Show that the likely attenders are supporters of your organisation (e.g. they attend several times a year)
You have got a fresh project idea that you think your existing audiences will support	• Collect feedback through a customer questionnaire • Ask people to express their opinion through your website • Conduct some telephone interviews to test customer demand

HINTS&TIPS

There are lots of sources of information about audiences and their attendance, or intended attendance at the arts. This information can help you build a case, support a funding application, provide stronger evidence to help you devise your strategic approach, or give you detailed information to form the basis of your marketing campaign.

Sources of information include:

Government departments and agencies

The 2001 Census .... www.statistics.gov.uk

Arts Council England .... www.artscouncil.org.uk/

Scottish Arts Council .... www.scottisharts.org.uk/

Arts Council of Wales .... www.artswales.org.uk/

These websites will have details of your local office

Museums, Libraries and Archives Council .. www.mla.gov.uk

This website will have details of your local office

Your local arts marketing agency .... www.audiencedevelopment.org

This website will have details of your local office

Other arts organisations

Previous research that has been done at your organisation

Your box office and other databases

 YOU DO IT

TARGET AUDIENCES

Identify your key target audiences. It might be helpful to define your existing target audience groups and the new target audiences. Use the areas of commonality listed at the start of the chapter to draw a picture of each group you have identified. Use the information you have gathered about each group to make realistic assumptions when setting numeric targets.

Check back to your marketing objectives, see p.20, to make sure your target audiences reflect the aims you have set out

[**REFER TO 3.1 OF SAMPLE MARKETING PLAN P. 66**]

TAKING IT FURTHER

Using information that is already available is cost-effective and can be quick and easy. If you need particular information that is not already available, you may need to consider commissioning your own research project.

Refer to:

Liz Hill *Commissioning Market Research*

Arts Council England *Information Sheet: Research*

WHAT MATTERS TO MY CUSTOMERS?

Now that we know who we want to talk to, and what their priorities and interests are, it becomes easier to identify what it is that those people would like from their arts experience.

Consider the following:

If you come to the football match you will see 22 men passing a ball between them with the aim of kicking it through a goal.

OR

The atmosphere at a match is electric. Even if you've never been before you'll be shouting yourself hoarse as you encourage your team to win. The crowd is always friendly and it won't be long before you're chanting and enjoying a beer with new friends.

The first paragraph tells you the key features of a football match, but conveys nothing of the experience of attending a match. The second paragraph manages, in a few words, to convey the benefits of attending that match: you get involved, you're welcomed, you might make new friends, your emotions will be engaged.

This process of trying to make the link between your activity and the things that really matter to audiences is known as identifying the "benefits" rather than the "features" of your activity.

Our challenge is to find ways of conveying the excitement and impact of the arts experience as much as describing the activity itself. Audience members are looking for all sorts of outcomes from an arts experience.

To begin, we must be aware that audiences don't just consider the artistic product when they are making their decisions. There are a whole variety of other factors that they will be concerned with, such as:

- *Will I be bored?*
- *Will I feel stupid?*
- *Will the people I take enjoy it?*
- *Is there somewhere to park?*
- *Does it fit into my schedule?*
- *Is it relevant to my life?*
- *Will it interest my friends when I tell them about it afterwards?*

As well as experiencing some art, audiences might also be looking for:

Learning

"I wanted to know more about the Second World War, I thought this exhibition would give me a different insight."

Participation

"I want something I can do with my children."

Inspiration and personal development

"These photographs of flowers make me want to spend more time in my garden."

Relaxation

"Learning a new skill like pottery helps me take my mind off my day to day."

Association and social opportunities

"I love coming to the venue, I always feel welcome. It's like I fit in, I feel at home."

CASE STUDY

"Daytime patrons can pick up their lunch and sample some of the best Italian coffee in town, but when the evening comes, it's the home of the best cocktail menu in the city. With summertime revellers able to bask in the evening sun on the outdoor tables and chairs, intermezzo is a truly cosmopolitan experience."
Mark Dobson, Tyneside Cinema

CASE STUDY

"Through the dance residency participants, parents and teachers got the chance to experience something new. They wanted to be part of something fun, exciting and professional yet at the same time also learn about the South Asian culture. We asked the artist to talk to the attenders during the performance about style of dance and the relationship of the 'Monsoon' concept to the South Asian culture.

It was a fantastic feeling to see so many people from mixed backgrounds and age groups really excited and enthused by the vibrancy and professionalism of the performance. Every single person involved with the performance felt a sense of achievement with what they had accomplished."
Rehana Amin, Art Asia

It can sometimes take a bit of lateral thinking to work out how to phrase features as benefits. Take inspiration from other marketing materials, for example holiday brochures, supermarket advertising or mortgage providers. Try to express what people will get out of your event: how will they feel, what will they learn and what can they share with others?

 YOU DO IT

KEY MESSAGES

Use the Target Audiences/Benefits Matrix (see p.57) to identify what aspects of your work will appeal to particular audiences. Use this information to formulate four or five key messages that encapsulate the most significant benefits. Include the completed grid as an appendix to your marketing plan.

[**REFER TO 3.2 OF SAMPLE MARKETING PLAN P. 68**]

HOW DO WE MAKE SURE WE'RE SAYING THE RIGHT THING TO THE RIGHT PEOPLE?

By considering the needs of our target audience and the benefits we have got to offer we can identify what messages we need to convey to which audiences.

You can develop some key messages that will appeal to your broad audiences, as well as more specific messages that will appeal more to people with a specialist or particular interest. Ensure that your messages are consistent with each other and with your own brand values.

CASE STUDY

"We are a hip hop collective doing breakin' and other hip hop art forms in street settings and theatres. With our show 'Stone Seeds' we wanted to reach two different audiences: a younger clubbing audience that enjoys breaking, but doesn't normally go to the theatre, and contemporary dance and ballet audiences that wouldn't necessarily consider breakin' as a valid theatre dance form. In order to reach these two diverse audiences we devised a dual publicity campaign, with one flyer aimed at a clubbing audience, and one at the dance/theatre audience."
Vivienne Perry, Sin Cru

TAKING IT FURTHER

Being customer-focused can represent a significant shift in the whole organisation's approach to its work. Many organisations have gone through this process and their stories may inspire you and your organisation.

Refer:

Morton Smyth *Not for the Likes of You:* Document A — How to Reach a Broader Audience, & Document B — Success Stories

HOW DO I KNOW HOW SUCCESSFUL WE WILL BE?

At the heart of a successful marketing plan are realistic audience targets. So far, everything we have done is based on assumptions about the audience and potential audience. Pulling together accurate information can help you set targets that the whole organisation is happy with, and that you (the person responsible for marketing) are confident can be achieved.

It is in your best interests to suggest achievable and realistic targets. It is easier to have difficult conversations about targets at the planning stage, and setting appropriate targets means you are more likely to succeed than fail.

When setting targets you should be as specific as possible. Ensure this by making them SMART (see p.19). Marketing targets tend to relate to the number of people who will attend or the amount of income you will generate from them.

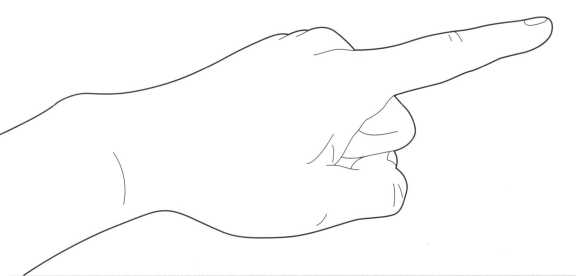

TARGET	SMART TARGET
We want to attract new audiences	• 25% of attenders for this event will not have visited us before
We want to attract family audiences	• 15% of visits will be by family groups consisting of one or more parents (or guardians or grandparents) with two or more children
We will raise more money on this event than we did last year	• We will increase income by 15% over last year

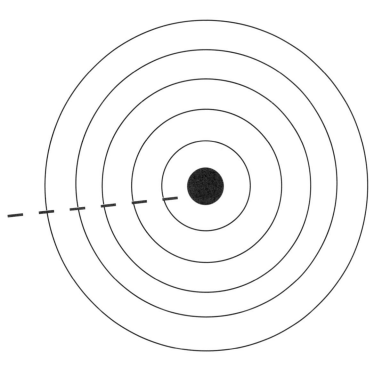

 YOU DO IT

OUR AUDIENCE TARGETS

For each of your target audience groups you can set a SMART target. Identify how many of them you aim to attract, and, if relevant, how much money you expect to generate from their attendance (other things you might want to set targets for include visit times, good qualitative feedback, repeat visits, etc.).

Ensure that these targets are consistent with the strategy you have set (e.g. set conservative targets with lower income levels for new audiences compared to existing audiences). Check that if you achieve these targets you will also achieve the SMART objectives you set earlier.

[**REFER TO 3.3 OF SAMPLE MARKETING PLAN P. 69**]

5 HOW WILL WE REACH THEM?

In this chapter we will be looking at how you choose your marketing tools to deliver cost-effective and efficient marketing campaigns.

WHAT'S IN THE MIX?

"The Marketing Mix" is a commonly used term which refers to the combination of activities that an organisation uses to achieve its objectives.

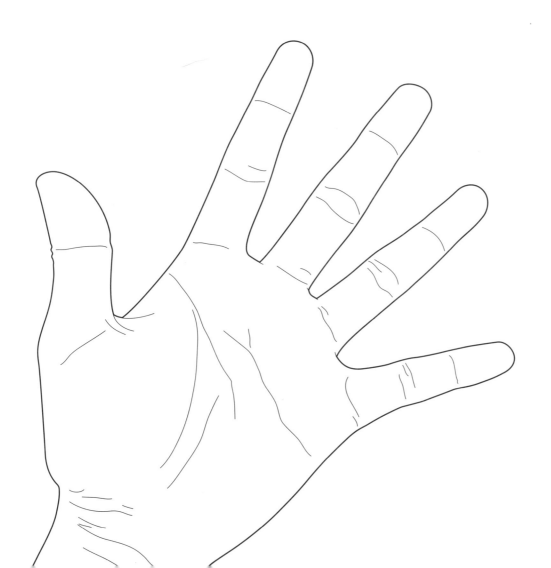

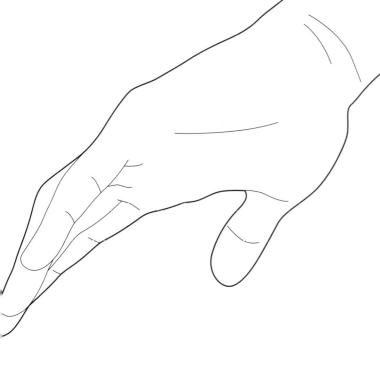

Getting the mix of activities right is crucial in making sure that you are talking to the right person at the right time about the right things and in a way that they will respond to.

The mix is basically a checklist to make sure that you have considered the key things that customers consider when making a decision. For this reason it is also sometimes known as the 4 Ps, where the Ps stand for Product, Price, Place and Promotion, or even the 7 Ps (adding on, People, Processes and Physical evidence). Some of the mix elements are more relevant to arts organisations than others, and this chapter considers a brief checklist to cover the key areas for your marketing plan. The areas we will consider are:

• your events and activities

• how much to charge

• your customers' experience and

• marketing tools.

DEVELOPING YOUR EVENTS AND ACTIVITIES

Earlier we talked about imagining your offer from the audiences' point of view (see p. 31), showing that your audience might consider other elements, such as merchandise, food and drink, programmes and facilities, as well as the artistic activity, as an important part of the experience.

As part of the marketing plan you should identify which elements of this experience need to be developed, changed or removed to appeal to your target audiences.

This is also an area where you are likely to be able to easily provide your customers with 'added value'. This term refers to anything that gives the customer something a little bit extra to what they might expect to get from the experience or purchase. They also serve to distinguish you from your competitors. Added value activities shouldn't cost you much to deliver (as you don't want to dent your profitability with non-essential extras), and should relate directly to what the recipient really values. Pre-show talks or gallery talks are a great example, because audience members value the opportunity to talk to the artist as well as the opportunity to learn more.

TAKING IT FURTHER

The marketing mix is an important marketing concept and it might be useful to familiarise yourself with it to develop your marketing plan further or if you are presenting it to others, e.g. your board.

Refer to:

Chartered Institute of Marketers
Ten-minute Guide: The Marketing List

CASE STUDY

"Our intention with Paradise Dreaming was to involve the audience by making them feel like they were guests at a wedding. Instead of giving them a ticket to enter the performance space, we gave them flowers to wear as buttonholes. They could choose pink to join the bride's party or blue for the groom's. Everyone was excited by being involved in this way, and the flowers added to their sense of unity as a wedding party. People have told us that they've kept the buttonholes as a keepsake of their enjoyable night out."
Sally Rew, HamFisted!

TAKING IT FURTHER

If you are writing a marketing plan for an organisation or programme that has several strands, it is worth considering the relationship between the elements of your programme in more detail.

Refer to:

Stephen Cashman ***Thinking Big!***
p. 45–48

HOW MUCH SHOULD I CHARGE?

Setting your prices can be a powerful tool in ensuring that you attract the customers you want. The key thing to bear in mind is that customers decide if a price is appropriate not just by how much cash they have got 'in their pocket' but how much they think the product or experience is worth.

So when choosing prices bear in mind whether or not you are offering good value. The sorts of things to consider include the following:

- Does your product fulfil the criteria of 'a good night out'?

- Is there a good chance that people will enjoy themselves, or are you asking them to take a risk?

- Is the product pricing comparable to the other things they might have done with that time? (Consider the wide range of competitive options, see p.15)

- Will your product provide a social opportunity, for example a birthday treat or to spend time with friends?

- Does the product have a significance or credibility to a certain audience group that makes it "unmissable"?

- Will the audience be able to talk about it afterwards, will the experience buy them social or cultural status?

- Is it rare or unique?

- Will the activity fulfil any of the participants' learning or educational needs?

Even if you are not planning to charge for your activity or event, you should consider the impact of perceived value on your customers.

Offering free access is often a successful way of maximising the numbers you can engage with your activity. However, when planning to make an event free you should consider value implications. Free can sometimes be equated with low value or low quality. Your marketing messages should be clear and promote the value of the opportunity you are providing.

Free activities can often give rise to low commitment. "I've had a free ticket for that show but it was raining and I couldn't be bothered to go out." If you're promoting a free activity it's important to reinforce the value and to encourage some sort of commitment from your audience.

DEVELOPING YOUR CUSTOMERS' EXPERIENCE

Every contact a customer or potential customer has with your organisation can impact on their impression of you and, ultimately, whether or not they want to engage with you. This means that the marketing plan needs to consider and manage all of those potential contact points. It also means that everyone involved with the organisation, staff members, board members, artists and volunteers will have a part in ensuring that the customer has the best possible impression of the organisation.

When you start to consider them, you'll find that there are a myriad of factors that affect your audience's opinion of you. Some of these factors may feel like they are in the hand of a third party – for example, if you sell your tickets through an external box office. Your plan should consider what you can do to positively affect the messages your third party suppliers, and the media, give about you.

CASE STUDY

"As a company touring productions for young people, we rely on the venues that we are visiting to attract young people, families and schools to the venue. In addition to the usual marketing and box office information about each show, we also offer specialist training to front-of-house staff to give them the skills and confidence to interact positively with groups of young people and provide recommendations about signage and dressing the venue depending on the age range of the show."
Frederica Notley, Pop-Up

To focus your thoughts it might be helpful to run through the following checklist, which should spark ideas about managing customer contact points.

Think about your *PEOPLE*

Consider all staff, artists, volunteers and others who come into contact with your customers (or potential customers).

* Are they sufficiently trained?
* Do they have the correct information?
* Are they the right people?
* Are they presented appropriately?

Think about your *PLACES*

Consider all places associated with your organisation including offices, performance or gallery spaces and other contact points (e.g. shops that sell your tickets).

* Is the venue the right one for the audience?
* Is it appropriately equipped?
* Is it physically accessible?
* Can people find the buildings easily?
* How easy it is to find their way around?

Think about your *PROCESSES*

Consider all your systems that might affect a customer experience – for example, the response they get when they phone you, your system for making reservations or bookings, or your system for customer complaints or comments.

* Are your systems aimed at making life easier for the customer or for you?
* Do customers get a quick, efficient response?
* Is it easy for customers to find out the information they need?
* Can people find their way around your systems easily?

Think about your *IDENTITY*

Does every customer contact point convey the values that you've identified as defining your organisation? Consider whether your activities sustain and reinforce your brand. Are you consistent and authentic in everything you do?

 YOU DO IT

AREAS FOR DEVELOPMENT

Get a team together to identify all the different ways a customer can come into contact with your organisation. You can use the Resource sheet: Customer Focus (p. 58) to structure the discussion. At the end you should have a list of areas of customer contact and an idea of which are good and which need improving.

[**REFER TO 4.1 OF SAMPLE MARKETING PLAN P. 70**]

Having a clear picture of your customer contact points gives you an understanding of your opportunities to influence an individual's impression of your organisation. They can be integrated into your marketing planning to ensure that you are proactive in managing your relationship with your customers.

CASE STUDY

"Our exhibitions encourage all visitors to find understanding through play and other activities. The Gallery's friendly and knowledgeable staff, especially the art interpreters, talk to all that come in.
We are well known for our ground-breaking interpretation for exhibitions and the stimulating interactives to help all enjoy and explore."
**Julie Davies,
Wolverhampton
Art Gallery**

USING MARKETING TOOLS

Often the selection of marketing tools is the thing people think about first when considering the marketing of their events and activities. I hope that the work we have done so far has shown that, in fact, your marketing tools are only part of a bigger picture. They are a crucial part, though, and we will now spend a bit of time working on how to put together the right set of tools for your needs.

There are a whole range of marketing tools that we commonly use to promote arts activities. The ones that usually jump to mind include:

• Flyers, posters, e-flyers, websites, direct mail and press coverage. These will probably be the major elements in your campaigns, but don't forget to consider other communications tools that might be useful to you, such as:

• Telephone marketing, Christmas cards, newsletters, events, giveaways, networking, advertising, sponsorship, SMS, podcasts and blogs. Last, but definitely not least, is the most elusive, but potentially most powerful marketing tool at your disposal, word of mouth.

HINTS&TIPS

WORD OF MOUTH

Talk to people

Word of mouth is the single most effective way of generating audiences. You don't have to cross your fingers and hope people are saying nice things about you – you can generate it yourself. Visit other events and talk to audience members, talk to people in the office buildings near you, or arrange informal visits to community groups, youth centres or other places where people meet and talk. You'll be surprised how many people will come to an event if they've been asked personally by someone with a genuine interest in their opinion.

Use your friends

Performers, artists, members of youth groups and even your core audience, can all be encouraged to proactively advocate for your organisation. You can use this resource effectively by ensuring that they are all well briefed and understand how they can help you achieve your audience aims. Consider inviting them to a rehearsal, or to see a presentation of forthcoming work. Invest in some hospitality and talk to them about their genuine reactions to the work. These people won't lie for you, but if they like what they see and feel that their opinion is valued they can become outspoken and positive advocates within their peer groups.

With such a variety of tools you have to select which to use, by considering which will work best with the audiences you want to attract.

Each of the tools identified has distinctive features which affect your choice for a particular activity. There are two broad categories, those which help us communicate with:

- a large number of people through a broad access medium, or

- directly with a selected individual.

Some of the tools we commonly work with straddle both these categories. For example, websites often fit into the "broad reach" category because they offer the same information to everyone who visits. Some of the most successful websites have adopted a more "targeted" approach to maximise their relationship with each visitor. For example, major online retailers often use your profile to make targeted offers on subsequent visits to their site.

An effective marketing campaign selects the most appropriate tools to reach its target audiences.

	BROAD REACH	**TARGETED**
The features of these tools	Aimed at a mass audience Have high visibility Convey simple generic messages	Aimed at an individual Have high relevance Convey a targeted message to the recipient
Examples	Outdoor media Newspaper advertising Sponsorship deals	Direct mail Targeted e-mails Telephone marketing
Cost	Relatively expensive (can be very expensive) Relatively quick to set up	Cost-effective when aimed at a carefully selected target group Relatively quick to set up
The results you can expect	A large number of people see your message High public profile Relatively low response rate	Fewer people see your message, but they're the people who count Little impact on public profile Higher response rate
Use them when	What you are promoting has a high recognition factor, for example a 'star' performer or a well-established brand	You have established a relationship with the individual that allows you to match your message to their interests

 YOU DO IT

TARGET AUDIENCES

You have already identified your target audiences (see p. 30), and you can use this list for the exercise below.

Fill in the Target Audiences/Communications Matrix you will find in the Resource Pack (p. 59). Working with a team can help get some fresh perspectives. Filling in the matrix can be a fun and engaging session that gets everyone thinking about audiences.

[**REFER TO 4.2 OF SAMPLE MARKETING PLAN P. 71**]

Having identified which tools you think will be most effective for attracting your desired target audiences, the next task is to use all the information you have collected to build a realistic campaign plan, which takes into account:

• how many people you want to attract

• how much money you've got to spend

• how much time you've got available

• accessibility of any other resources you need.

Once you have put together your outline plan you are in a position to pull together an outline budget and timeline for your campaign. In the next chapter we will look at this practical implementation of your plans and how to build on your successes in the future.

TAKING IT FURTHER

There is a wealth of information available to help you to build robust campaign plans, and to make effective use of marketing tools.

Refer to:

Liz Hill *Creative Arts Marketing*

Heather Maitland *The Marketing Manual*

Daniel Hadley *Boost Your Performance:* Writing your Marketing Action Plan pp.16–22

6 HOW DO WE MAKE THE MOST OF THE PLAN?

In this chapter we will be looking at ensuring that your strategy can be delivered within your resources in a timely manner and how you can use your experience to inform future activity

HOW CAN I ENSURE THAT THE PLAN IS DELIVERABLE?

Now that you know exactly what it is you want to do, the time has come to be specific about when you're going to do it and how much it is going to cost.

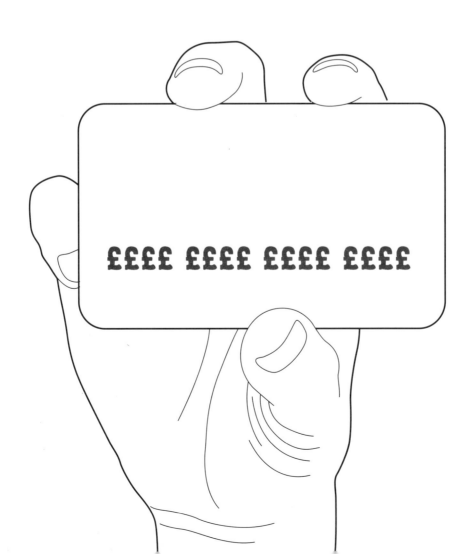

HOW DO I KNOW HOW MUCH TO SPEND?

With the information you have now gathered it should be a fairly simple task to put together your marketing budget.

A significant part of the budget will be made up of the direct costs that are associated with the marketing campaign plan you have written. In this part of the budget you can cost all the activity you have planned. Be as precise as possible and use actual costs to put together your budget, for example:

TOOL	DETAIL	NUMBER	UNIT COST	TOTAL
Direct mail				
	Target group A	70 letters	33p	£23
	Target group B	190 letters	33p	£63
	Casual staff to stuff letters	2 hours	£6	£12

In addition to the campaign costs, don't forget to include figures for the other activities you've identified in your marketing plan. They might not all need money (many will just take time) but ensuring that you have enough financial resources available will help ensure that you have the capacity to do all the things you want to.

Examples of the sorts of things that might need to be costed out are:

- website developments
- corporate print
- signage
- research
- special events
- new IT resources (e.g. data collection systems)

HINTS&TIPS

WHAT YOU CAN GET FOR LITTLE OR NO MONEY

When planning your marketing it helps your money go further if you include activities that cost little or no money. Free things are often more resource-hungry though – for example, press coverage is free, but it can require a large investment in staff time to get the story you want in the place you want to see it.

Build partnerships

Working with others is one of the best ways of cutting costs. Identify other arts organisations with similar target audiences and negotiate shared mailings or swap programme ads. Giving out flyers as an audience leaves another event is often a good way to get directly to your target audience – make sure you discuss what you want to do with the other venue first!

You can also work with organisations in different sectors. For example, link with a local transport company by offering to promote their services to your customers if they will promote your events on their vehicles.

E-marketing

Sending e-mails is extremely cheap and it is easy to encourage others to forward them on for you. Recipients are much more likely to read an e-mail from a trusted source, so build up a contacts list of influential people who will forward your e-mails on.

Word of mouth

Time-intensive but extremely effective, word of mouth is hard to control and often feels like it is completely out of our hands. However, it can also be a powerful tool that you can influence and plan into your campaign (see p.41).

HOW DO I KNOW WHEN TO DO THINGS?

To ensure that you have enough time to deliver all the elements of your marketing plan it is helpful to prepare a timeline.

The usual technique is to start at the event date (or other deadline) and count backwards for activity. For example, if you would like your customers to receive their brochure three weeks before the start of a season you will have to ensure that the stuffed envelopes are ready about four weeks prior to the start of the season, which will mean the brochures need to be delivered five weeks prior and so on.

While planning your timeline ensure that you take into account staff holidays, public holidays, availability of casual staff and anything else that might affect your ability to deliver to time. Leave a good margin when setting deadlines to help ensure you meet them.

WEEK COMMENCING	ACTIVITY AREA	DETAIL	WHO'S RESPONSIBLE
1st April	Pricing policy	Present ideas for autumn season pricing plan	Me
	Children's workshops promotion	Direct mail to previous attenders	Me
	Events brochure	Gather final information from artists	Andy
8th April	Children's workshops promotion	Children's workshops leaflets to nurseries	Andy
	Children's workshops promotion	Agree snacks and refreshments available to workshop attenders	Lucy
15th April	Main brochure	Write copy, including new pricing information	Me

There are no hard-and-fast rules that govern how far in advance of an event you should implement activities within your campaign. Your detailed understanding of your target audiences will help you select the time that will have the best chance of success – you can consider how far in advance they are likely to make their decisions and what information they will need available to make that decision.

"We tailor the timing of the release of information about our event according to the audience. For example, we want teachers to bring groups of pupils to see some of the shows in our programme. We ensure that information is sent out before the start of term to allow them time to plan their term time schedule and all the administration that goes with organising a school outing."
Ranjit Atwal, The Old Town Hall

 YOU DO IT

BUDGET AND TIMETABLE

Using the examples above, write a budget and a timeline for your marketing campaign. Ensure you include any activities you decided to carry out when considering your "marketing mix" (see p.36) as well as all the marketing tools you want to use.

[**REFER TO 4.3 AND 4.4 OF SAMPLE MARKETING PLAN P.72 AND P.73**]

HOW DO I KNOW IF IT'S WORKING?

Your budget and your timeline are two important tools for ensuring that your plan stays on track and delivers what you need it to. To maintain buy-in from the team you are working with, it is helpful to arrange regular meetings were everybody can feedback on their progress. This will help you spot problems in advance or unexpected successes, and change your plans accordingly.

WHAT HAVE I LEARNT FOR NEXT TIME?

Marketing is a learning process. What works for one organisation may not work for others. Your marketing plan is very unlikely to turn out exactly as you expected – maybe you don't quite achieve all you intended, maybe things take off and your expectations are exceeded.

The discrepancies between predictions and actuality can be the result of something completely unexpected and unpredictable. For example, no one expected the Birmingham tornado of 2005, a freak weather occurrence that brought the city to a complete standstill.

More often, we find that more precise assumptions or accurate information could have allowed us to refine our forecasts more closely. For example, the World Cup had a significant impact on people's leisure time in June and July 2006, whether or not they were football fans. Successful organisations built this into their marketing plans.

We can learn to be more accurate in our marketing predictions by ensuring that we compare the actuality against our targets and analyse why the discrepancies arose. You can feed this information into the next marketing plan, and refine your activity building on what you know works for you.

Your main evaluation should be to check whether you are achieving the SMART targets you set out earlier in your plan, and whether these targets are helping you reach the marketing objectives you set right at the start of the plan.

You will be able to use this information to plan the next campaign. It will be more accurate than the "folk memory", and will be even more helpful when there has been a changeover in staff, which could otherwise result in information being lost.

Throughout this planning process we have been including a broad team of staff, board, volunteers, artists and other associates to contribute to the planning and delivery of this campaign. Bring everyone involved together once it's over to assess how well you have met your objectives. Congratulate each other on your successes and use the meeting as a springboard to continuing the good work!

 YOU DO IT

EVALUATION TOOLS

Write an evaluation plan using the template above. Incorporate any activity you identify, such as printing special offer vouchers, into your timeline, to make sure you've got time to make them happen.

[**REFER TO 5.1 AND 5.2 OF SAMPLE MARKETING PLAN P.74**]

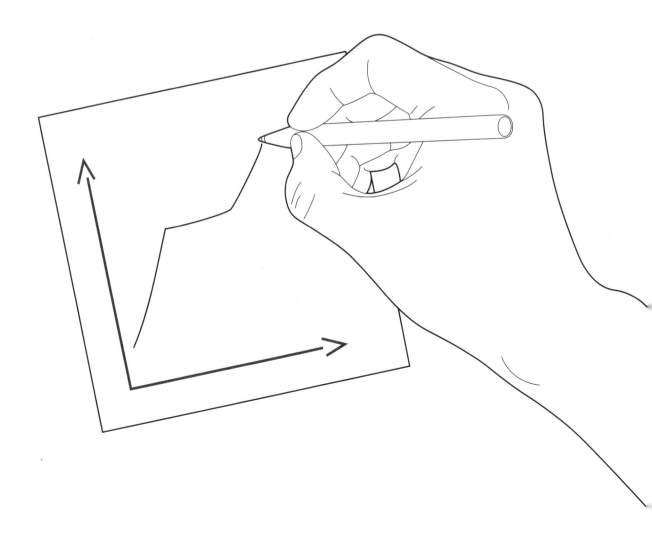

HOW CAN WE ENSURE OUR PLAN WORKS?

In this chapter we'll look at ways of ensuring that the plan doesn't sit on a shelf but is adopted and used by the whole organisation.

WHAT ARE THE LONG-TERM BENEFITS?

Your marketing plan helps your organisation to be successful by providing a management structure for your relationship with your audiences. To be effective, the plan needs to impact on the work of the whole organisation. <u>Everyone involved has to play their role in the implementation of the plan.</u>

For the plan to have the best chance of success you need to ensure that everyone is involved in its development – from the overarching direction to the detailed delivery mechanisms. Throughout this book we have outlined opportunities to include staff, board members, volunteers, artists, audiences and other stakeholders, to contribute to the development of the marketing plan. These opportunities can help to get everyone behind the plan, as well as to ensure you have considered a wide range of options and opinions when making decisions about your relationship to your audiences.

HINTS&TIPS

GETTING BUY-IN FROM THE TEAM

There are some common sticking points that occur when writing your marketing plan. Here are some examples and suggestions on how to get the team involved in resolving them.

Unrealistic audience expectations

Will audiences turn up in the numbers anticipated, or will you really be able to engage a new audience?

• Use previously gathered information from similar events to draw comparisons

• Keep a log of marketing activity alongside event numbers so that you can correlate and cost marketing activity for similar outcome

• Use up-to-date information, such as box office data or your records of previous attendance, to make realistic estimates of potential audience numbers

• Suggest setting conservative targets to provide a buffer

Differing perceptions of the audience's understanding of the organisation and its activity

Is there a difference between what the audience thinks of the organisation and what the organisation thinks of itself?

• Try the branding exercise in the Resource Pack, pp.55–56. Try it with a range of different people, e.g. staff, board, supporters, audience members, etc. This tool helps everybody take a broad approach to the positive and negative perceptions people might have about your organisation

• Try a customer survey to get some accurate feedback

• Get team members to talk to customers – give them a mission to find out a particular piece of information

The organisation is reluctant to question the product

Is this a reluctance in the organisation to include thoughts about the audience in the development of the art or the product?

• Get team members to think about the 'whole' experience, including arrival, welcome, facilities

• Work with the team to set realistic targets (see p.30).

Others question the marketing approach

Does the organisation focus on visible campaigns (e.g. press profile or leaflet distribution) and have less regard for other mechanisms (e.g. direct mail, advocacy)?

• Involve everyone in identifying target audiences and the features of the product

• Plan a budget to share with the team that indicates where spend is going to be focused

• Work with the team to identify clear targets and demonstrate the spread of marketing activity to achieve these targets

IT'S AS SIMPLE AS THAT

You've made it to the end of your marketing plan!

I hope that the tools and ideas in this book have enabled you to build a plan that accurately reflects the aims and objectives of your organisation, and provides a clear action plan for achieving them.

The process described has encouraged you to include colleagues, board members, associates, artists and audiences, as you've prepared your plan. Their involvement will help you to ensure that the plan is deliverable and everyone feels they have a crucial role in forming and maintaining happy and healthy relationships with audiences.

Congratulations on taking your organisation through this process and producing your marketing plan. Good luck!

RESOURCE PACK

This section contains additional resources to help you complete your plan, including exercises, further reading and a sample

RESOURCES

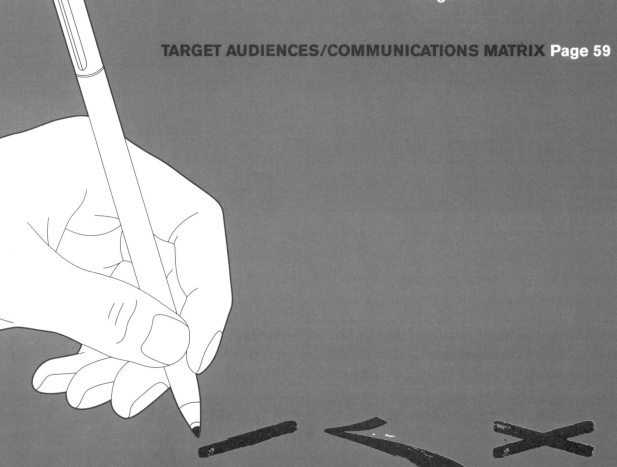

BRANDING EXERCISE
(ADAPTED FROM AN AMA MODEL)

This exercise is a great way of identifying the key values that characterise your organisation. Ask people to:

1. Circle the words (good or bad) that you believe currently describe the organisation.

2. Put a + next to those words circled that you believe to be positive and a - next to those words you would ideally like to change.

3. Look at the words not circled and put a * next to any words that you think you'd like the organisation to be described as in the future.

4. Compare notes and probe people as to why they have selected certain words. This should open up a discussion about what you would like to keep and what you would like to change about the way the organisation is perceived.

Try it with a range of different people, e.g. other staff, board, suppliers, designers, audience members, visitors, etc.

Aggressive	Diverse	Innovative	Proactive
Approachable	Downmarket	Inspiring	Progressive
Arrogant	Dynamic	Jolly	Professional
Assured	Easy-going	Kind	Quiet
Attractive	Elegant	Knowledgeable	Quirky
Beautiful	Elitist	Lazy	Reactive
Bright	Entertaining	Leisurely	Relaxed
Broad-minded	Experienced	Loyal	Reputable
Careful	Fair-minded	Mature	Secretive
Cheeky	Fashionable	Moody	Selfish
Clean	Fresh	Naïve	Serious
Cold	Friendly	Narrow-minded	Show-off
Comfortable	Genuine	Nervous	Sophisticated
Condescending	Grand	Obliging	Sympathetic
Confident	Haughty	Ordinary	Traditional
Conventional	High-class	Ostentatious	Trend setting
Determined	Immature	Patronising	Unusual
Disorganised	Impressive	Phoney	Vain
Distinctive	Inconsistent	Pretentious	Welcoming

NOTE: EXPAND THIS LIST AS YOU FEEL RELEVANT

TARGET AUDIENCES/BENEFITS MATRIX

Enter your target audiences across the top axis and your benefits down the side axis.

Tick the top three benefits for each target audience. You will see which benefits (the most ticked) are the most important for you to convey broadly and which will be particularly important to specific target groups.

TARGET AUDIENCES

BENEFITS

CUSTOMER FOCUS EXERCISE

You can do this exercise alone, but getting other team members involved will help get buy-in from everyone. Include staff members and board members (if appropriate). You can also invite 'supportive friends' – these might be audience members or other supporters of the organisation.

Stage 1

Break your team into small groups and lead them through the following questions. Give them enough time to write down their responses to each.

How do they hear about your work?

Put as much detail as possible into the answer here. If they heard about it on the radio, which station and what was said?

What is their experience when they phone you?

Did they get through quickly? Was the response welcoming? Was the person who answered the call knowledgeable and able to answer their queries? What happens if there is no one to answer the phone?

How did they find your website?

Was the information they needed clearly accessible? Was the website accessible? Is the copy on the website clear and easy to read? Was it welcoming?

What do they think when they pick up your flyer?

Was the information they needed clearly accessible?

If they were handed the flyer, was the distributor able to answer their questions? Were they polite?

What is their experience when they arrived?

Did they feel welcome? Was the signage clear? Did they know where to go? Could they access the facilities they needed, e.g. toilets, baby-changing units?

What impact does your building give?

Does the building look welcoming and friendly? Can people find their way around it? Does it invite people to enter? Is it clear what goes on inside?

What happens after they've attended an event?

What will they remember? Do they have anything to take away with them? Do they feel that you would like to see them again?

Stage 2

Assign each group one of your target customer groups and ask them to revisit their answers from their point of view.

Stage 3

Summarise by identifying areas that will need development to meet the needs of the target audiences.

TARGET AUDIENCES/COMMUNICATIONS MATRIX

Enter your target audiences across the top axis and your communications tools down the side axis.

Tick the top three most effective communications tools for each target audience. Circle the one that you think will be the most useful way of communicating with that audience.

TARGET AUDIENCES

COMMUNICATIONS

SAMPLE MARKETING PLAN

This sample marketing plan, based on an imaginary arts organisation, is provided to give you an idea of what a plan might look like and how the information fits together.

Use the  YOU DO IT throughout the book to help you create a plan for your own organisation, campaign or project.

[SAMPLE]

THIS SAMPLE MARKETING PLAN IS PROVIDED AS A GUIDE ONLY. YOU MIGHT LIKE TO GO INTO MORE DETAIL OR PROVIDE ADDITIONAL INFORMATION WHEN WRITING YOUR OWN PLAN.

1. OUR ORGANISATION

1.1
WHO WE ARE

[REFER TO P.13]

Sing Your Heart Out exists to instil the love of opera in young people from an early age by making it a part of their everyday lives.

We have a small team of two full-time and one part-time member of staff.

We work with children aged 11–16 in schools within the city throughout the year.

We produce an annual performance of a classic opera, using a cast of professional singers and young people from the schools we are working with.

We aim to involve the local community in all our activities, including participation in workshops and performances and attendance at performances.

We are a not-for-profit organisation and a registered charity. Our financial aims are to generate enough income to be able to continue to deliver the sort of work we believe in. 70% of our income comes from funders who support our work in schools and our commitment to making excellent opera accessible. We raise the remaining 30% of our income through our annual performance.

Note:

Use your company's vision or mission statement, business plan and other strategic documents to inform this summary of your organisation.

1.2
WHAT OUR AUDIENCE THINKS OF US

[REFER TO SECTION ON "BRAND VALUES" ON P.13]

We believe opera is life-changing, emotive and significant. Watching and singing opera enhances people's lives and everyone can benefit from an opera experience.

Sing Your Heart Out is accessible, welcoming and tears down barriers between audiences and art.

Sing Your Heart Out produces top-quality work. We challenge the art establishment and traditional opera attenders with a quirky, contemporary interpretation of classic works.

Sing Your Heart Out can be relied on to see things in a new and unexpected way.

Sing Your Heart Out is dedicated to this city and its people. At the same time, the work is of national significance and we have a national profile.

Sing Your Heart Out makes opera that the local community can be involved with and enjoy.

[REFER TO SECTION ON "USP" ON P.14]

If we were to summarise what we think people think of us, it would be:

" Pioneering, exciting, quirky and exceptionally good opera that gets under your skin and encourages you to get involved."

Note:

Your USP will be just as effective expressed as a few dynamic bullet points if you are struggling to find one snappy sentence to encapsulate what you want to say.

1.3
WHAT'S HAPPENING AROUND US
[REFER TO SECTION ON "COMPETITORS" ON P.15]

Significant competitors for attendance at event

• Established traditional opera companies

• Other contemporary arts events

• Local street festival

Significant competitors for participation at workshops

• Youth centre

• Sports facilities and classes

• Family commitments

1.4
OUR STRENGTHS, WEAKNESSES, OPPORTUNITIES AND THREATS (SWOT)

[REFER TO SECTION ON "BRINGING IT ALL TOGETHER", ON P.16]

Strengths

Established reputation

Expertise

Few competitors

Committed staff team

Potential to attract major international artists

Weaknesses

Small staff team

Inadequate office facilities

Limited marketing resources

Small fish in a pond with some big players

Financial resources are committed to our existing programme

Opportunities

Arts Council policy focusing on young people

Arts Council policy focusing on participation

Growth of interest in our work opera in local communities

Increased profile will help attract higher quality artists

Funding opportunities to engage young people with opera

Emerging partnerships with local theatre and education

Increased media interest in our organisation

Threats

Our main funders, resources may be cut

Local authority priorities are shifting to other art-forms

Health and Safety legislation may affect how we stage our shows

Reduction of music tuition within schools

SWOT Summary:

Over the next three years we aim to capitalise on the opportunities that the Arts Council's changes in policy are bringing. In order to do this we will need to focus staff resources on ensuring that the Arts Council, nationally and regionally, know about and understand our work.

The growth in our profile means that we should be able to make a big splash with our next production, by featuring one or more artists of internationally high status. We need to ensure that we have the financial resources to achieve this and that the marketing resources are in place to capitalise on the opportunity.

2. OUR STRATEGY

2.1
WHERE WE'RE HEADING

[**REFER TO SECTION ON "SETTING OBJECTIVES" ON P.20**]

- At least one child to take a major singing role in the annual event in three years' time

- Attract a major professional singer to perform at our annual event next year

- Increase the number of children from ethnically diverse backgrounds to participate in our workshops to 15%

- Increase the number of attenders from ethnically diverse backgrounds at our annual event from 0.5% to 5% in the next year, increasing to 10% in three years

- Increase attendance at our annual event from 70% to 90% in three years

- Raise an extra £2000 from the annual event in the next year, increasing by £500 per year for the next two years

- Involve at least 30 members of local community in workshops or annual performance

2.2
HOW WE'LL GET THERE

[REFER TO SECTION ON "MARKETING STRATEGIES" ON P.25]

STRATEGY FOR	DETAIL	WHO'S LEADING?
Our core work	Get to know our core attenders better and develop our activities to keep them engaged in the long term	Me
	Identify our core target market and undertake activity to grow it	Me
Develop the market	Invest in focused work with two key schools to ensure that we start to develop individual singers and performers with the potential to form careers in opera	Lucy
	Forge relationships with schools with a high percentage of South Asian and Afro-Caribbean children	Lucy
	Research market for opera attenders among South Asian and Afro-Caribbean communities	Me
	Develop relationships with local community groups, especially those in South Asian and Afro-Caribbean communities	Anne
Develop the product	Focus on developing national profile that stresses our excellence, uniqueness and quality	Me
	Start to form partnerships with opera companies and individual singers	Anne
	Lobby funders to provide resources to engage major opera stars	Anne

3. OUR AUDIENCES

3.1
TARGET AUDIENCES

[**REFER TO SECTION ON "TARGET AUDIENCES" ON P.30**]

The market opportunity

This is an ideal time for *Sing Your Heart Out* to be aiming to attract new attenders. Our raised profile, plus the decision to attract a major name star, means that we have an event that is unique in the city and which will appeal to existing opera attenders as well as people who have never attended opera before.

Our event is the only opera regularly staged in the city that is performed in English. This means we provide an essential experience for established and new audiences, who would find opera performed in other languages inaccessible.

Our press profile is evidence that our work is considered "unique" and "nationally significant" and as such it forms an important part of the arts picture of the city.

We have researched existing opera provision in the city and identified March as a month when there is no other professional opera activity available, making our event even more attractive to individuals who attend opera elsewhere.

Our core audiences

Keen opera attenders who are not opera purists

- Interested in unusual interpretations of classic opera as long as singing is top-quality

- 50+, married and whose children have moved away

- Attend with their partner and often with other couples

- Live in the affluent suburbs of the city

- Highly educated with professional career (maybe retired)

Friends and family of the participating children

- Interested in seeing their children or grandchildren perform

- No or little previous experience of opera

- Rarely attend any arts activity and rarely visit city centre for any reason

- Live on the estates surrounding the schools where we work

- Reliant on public transport

- 25–40, families made up of single parents and married couples; grandparents have important role in family life

- Variety of ethnic and cultural backgrounds; opera not necessarily an art-form that they feel is important to them

- Demographics of this group show they are more likely to use English as a second language, be in poor health, and be out of work, educated to secondary level with additional vocational qualifications.

School groups of children 11 and upwards who are studying music or drama

- Schools we are working with (or have worked with)
- Specialist performing arts schools

New audiences

Keen theatre or music attenders who are interested in something unusual

- Interested in unusual and artistically excellent interpretations of classic theatre or music
- People who are prepared to try something new
- Attend with friends or with their partner
- May have children they are interested in introducing to opera
- Live within 30 minutes' travel time of the venue
- Educated to degree level and working in professional career

Opera lovers from South Asian or Afro-Caribbean backgrounds

We currently know little about how large this target group is, and have no information about who they are or where they live. These individuals might be interested in attending events or participating in our activities. Our first task will be to undertake desk research to understand this group better.

Choosing the schools we work with

The schools we work with have a huge impact on the reach of all our activity, and relate to developing core audiences and new audiences.

We will identify one Performing Arts Specialist School that we already work with to enter into a three-year intensive partnership.

In addition, with two new schools per year, using the following selection criteria to ensure that the schools we select to work with will also help us reach our organisation objectives.

- High proportion of pupils from South Asian or Afro-Caribbean backgrounds
- Low provision of arts activity in the area
- Communities in geographic areas that are near, or have easy transport routes, to the likely location of the final production
- Community infrastructures that are open to partnership working
- Communities that have been identified by funders as of particular interest for development and engagement with the arts

3.2
KEY MESSAGES

[**REFER TO SECTION ON "SAYING THE RIGHT THINGS" ON P.33**]

- This is a one-off opportunity to see something unique, powerful, dramatic and exciting
- This is top-quality opera
- See something you know from a different perspective
- See your child performing with professionals
- A great night out for you and your family
- It's an easy way to introduce yourself to opera
- The show is in English
- You won't be bored
- A rich and stunning visual feast
- Your friends will thank you for introducing them to this
- Be part of something special

Note:

A completed Target Audiences/Benefits Matrix (available in the Resources Pack, p.57) helps reinforce your analysis. Include as an appendix to your marketing plan.

3.3
OUR AUDIENCE TARGETS

[REFER TO SECTION ON "OUR AUDIENCE TARGETS" ON P.35]

AUDIENCE GROUP	TARGET	INCREASED INCOME
Keen opera attenders	Increase by 20% per year and 10% per year for the next two years. (Average price of £15 per ticket.)	Year 1 400–480 £1200 Year 2 480–528 £720 Year 3 528–581 £795 181 more attendances £2751 more income
Friends and family	50 attendances by family and friends from each of the three schools we work with by year 2. (Average price of £5 per ticket, Performing Arts college; £2 per ticket other schools.)	We are already achieving 50 attendances from Performing Arts College For attendances from other schools @ £2 each Year 1 40–80 Year 2 80–100 60 more attendances £120 more per year
School groups	Two extra school groups of 20 pupils to attend this year (four groups in total). Four school groups in total in subsequent years. (School groups pay average of £4.50 per ticket.)	120 more attendances £540 more income
Keen theatre or music attenders	Attract 50 new attenders in this year. Additional 30 attenders per year for the following two years. (Average price of £12.50 per ticket)	110 new attendances £1375 more income
Opera lovers from South Asian or Afro-Caribbean backgrounds	Attract five new attenders in this year. Additional five attenders per year for the following two years. (Average price of £12.50 per ticket.)	15 new attenders £186 more income

This plan will deliver our financial objectives set out earlier (including a margin to allow for variations to plans).

OBJECTIVE	TOTALS FROM	ABOVE
Year 1	+£2000	£2508
Year 2	+£500	£1198
Year 3	+£500	£1233
Totals	+£3000	+£4939

4. IMPLEMENTATION PLAN

4.1
AREAS OF DEVELOPMENT

[**REFER TO SECTION ON "WHAT'S IN THE MIX?" ON P. 36**] This analysis was put together at a staff meeting that looked at the audiences' experiences of *Sing Your Heart Out.*

Area for development	Action	Responsible
Pricing: are we underselling the work to keen opera attenders?	Review pricing of other opera events and other theatre and music performances	Me
Booking tickets: not always easy to get through at the box office	Investigate online ticketing options and implement	Adi
Understanding our core audience	Identify who our core attenders are – talk to them to understand what they feel about us and what we do	Me
Visiting artists: not always able to control workshop groups	Prepare briefing pack for artists Ensure artist always has assistant and that the teacher is present throughout the session	Lucy
Disability access: venue is fully accessible – do customers know this?	Ensure all communications material is available in accessible formats Form partnership with local disability awareness forum to help promote the opportunity	Me
Professionalism: some people think we work primarily in schools and don't realise our shows are professional and top-quality	All press releases to contain information about professional work Education materials for pupils, teachers and parents to stress quality of professional work	Me Lucy
Participation: local participants hard to engage	Need to clarify messages for local participants Spend more time in locality at times when trying to engage participants	Me Anne

4.2
MARKETING TOOLS

[**REFER TO SECTION ON "USING MARKETING TOOLS" ON P. 41 AND "TARGET AUDIENCES" ON P. 43**]

Audience Group	Tools	Details
Keen opera attenders	Direct mail	Letter to our previous attenders and to external lists
	Flyers and posters	Distributed in residential areas and city centre
	Website	Promote online booking
	Press	Local radio and national print press – endorsing quality product
Friends and family	Flyers and posters	Distributed through children and at school
	Website	Focus on special offers Include beginners guide to this opera
	Word of mouth	Encourage teachers, pupils and parents to spread the word
School groups	Flyers and posters	Distributed directly to teachers
	Direct e-mail	Personal approach to named teachers
	Website	Develop special schools pack
	Word of mouth	Through artists and workshop leaders to teachers
Keen theatre or music attenders	Direct e-mail	To externally sourced e-mail lists Include special offer
	Direct mail	To externally sourced lists Include special offer
	Flyers and posters	Distributed in other venues and in city centre
Opera lovers from South Asian or Afro-Caribbean backgrounds	Direct e-mail	To externally sourced e-mail lists Include special offer
	Direct mail	To externally sourced lists Include special offer
	Word of mouth	Develop relationships with key influencers

Note: A completed Target Audiences/Benefits Matrix (Resources Pack, p.57) can be included as an appendix to support your plan.

4.3
BUDGET OVERVIEW

[**REFER TO SECTION ON "BUDGETING" ON P. 48**]

Tool	Detail	Unit Cost
Press	Hire press consultant	£1500
Website developments	Used to drive e-marketing campaigns	£500
	Online ticketing	£1000
Print	Flyers	£500
	Posters	£500
Design	Print and e-flyers	£400
Customer research	Gathering core customer opinions	£200
Direct mail	Price for postage and stuffing	£600
Distribution	Leaflets and flyers	£400
		Total £5600

4.4
TIMETABLE OVERVIEW

Activity Area	Detail	Who's responsible	When
Press	Develop new key messages for use in all material	Me	By September
Fundraising	Identify funds for major artist	Anne	By September
Partnership building	Identify new schools with high numbers of BME pupils	Lucy	By September
Schools work	Prepare artists information pack Prepare information pack for schools and parents	Lucy	By September
Participation	Local visits and presentations	Anne	By October
Ticketing	Investigate online products	Adi	By October
Communications	E-marketing campaign to schools with targeted materials	Me	November
Partnerships	Establish working partnership with new artists	Anne	By December
Press	Identify press consultant for national press campaign	Me	By December
Access	Disability audit	Me	By December
Pricing review	Check consistency with other local providers	Me	By December
Press	Agree national, regional and local press releases Launch national campaign	Me	January
Ticketing	Launch online ticket sales	Adi	January
Communications	Production of event flyer and posters Details of event on web	Me	January
Research	Core attenders	Me	By January
Research	BME opera attenders	Me	By January
Communications	Direct mail campaigns Distribution of event posters E-marketing campaigns Recruit ambassadors to generate word of mouth	Me	February
Press	Launch local and regional campaigns	Me	February

Note: Your budget and timetable can be presented as an overview in the plan. Use the techniques suggested on pp. 44–49 to produce more detailed action plans and attach them as appendices if required.

5. MONITORING AND EVALUATION

5.1
MONITORING OUR SUCCESS

The activity plans above will be used to monitor our success. Each has a timescale and a named staff member responsible for delivery.

Delivery of the plan will be monitored by the General Manager and will be a regular feature of our weekly staff meetings.

5.2
EVALUATION TOOLS

All activity in this plan will be reviewed in order to inform subsequent planning and target setting. Key elements for evaluation are:

Activity	Target	Future action
Press	Agree targets with press consultant. Must include some national press	Use information to set press budget for next year Decide what press activity can be undertaken in-house
Set up of online ticketing	10% ticket sales through the online system	Use information to develop service Customer feedback on usefulness Set higher online targets for next year
Research	Customer feedback from 20% of attenders	Use information to revise subsequent programmes and products
Pricing review	Implementation of new pricing structure for event in March	
Access	Disability access implementation plan written and on track	Measure achievements in April Activity planned for after this date on track
	Plan presented to the board	Timetable for annual revision of the plan set up and agreed by board
Audience and participation targets	Achieve targets outlined in Section 3 above	Review targets for years 2 and 3
Communications methods	Monitor all special offers Monitor success of all promotional methods	Review campaign planning for years 2 and 3 to focus on cost-effective and efficient techniques

The evaluation will be carried out by the General Manager and a report will be prepared after our event for presentation at our May board meeting.

REFERENCE MATERIALS

ONLINE RESOURCES

Arts Council England (ACE)
Information Sheet: Research
© May 2003 (updated November 2005)
www.artscouncil.org.uk

Chartered Institute of Marketers (CIM)
Ten-minute Guide: The Marketing List ©2004
www.cim.co.uk

Morton Smyth
Not For The Likes Of You © 2004
www.newaudiences.org.uk

PUBLICATIONS

Stephen Cashman
Thinking BIG! A Guide to Strategic Marketing Planning for Arts Organisations
© 2003 AMA

Daniel Hadley
Boost YOUR Performance: Writing your Marketing Action Plan
© 2001 Scottish Arts Council

Liz Hill
Commissioning Market Research: A Guide for Arts Marketers
© 2000 AMA

Liz Hill, Catherine O' Sullivan & Terry O'Sullivan
Creative Arts Marketing 2nd edition
© 2003 Butterworth Heinemann

Heather Maitland
The Marketing Manual
1990 (Revised 2000)
© AMA

Malcolm McDonald
Marketing Plans
© 1984 (Revised 1999) Butterworth Heinemann

Peter Verwey
Marketing Planning
1985 (Revised April 2006)
© Arts Council of Great Britain

NOTES